Data Science for Beginners

A Practical Guide to Getting Started

By Oluchi Ike

Preface:

Welcome to *Data Science for Beginners: A Practical Guide to Getting Started*. If you've ever been curious about how to make sense of the growing amount of data in the world or wondered how data-driven decisions are made, then you've picked the right book. Whether you're a student, a professional switching careers, or simply someone interested in learning what data science is all about, this guide will give you a solid foundation to start your journey.

Data science has rapidly become one of the most important fields across various industries—from business to healthcare to technology. Despite its growth, the concept can often feel intimidating, especially for beginners. This book aims to break down those barriers by explaining complex ideas in an easy-to-understand manner, offering step-by-step examples, and providing real-world projects that will help you apply what you learn.

We'll cover the essential tools and techniques you need to get started, including basic statistics, data cleaning, visualization, and simple machine learning models. Along the way, you'll be introduced to Python, one of the most popular programming languages for data science, and key libraries such as Pandas and Matplotlib.

This is not just a textbook but a practical guide. By the end of the book, you will have worked on projects that simulate real-world data science tasks, and you'll gain the confidence to pursue more advanced topics. The path to becoming a data scientist can be long, but with this guide, you'll take your first steps with clarity and direction.

Thank you for choosing this book. I'm excited to accompany you on this rewarding journey into the world of data science!

Happy learning!

Oluchi Ike

Table of Contents:

1. **Introduction to Data Science**

    o   What is Data Science?

    o   Why Data Science Matters

    o   The Data Science Workflow: From Data Collection to Insights

    o   Key Roles in Data Science: Data Scientist, Analyst, Engineer, and More

2. **Getting Started with Python for Data Science**

    o   Why Python? The Power of Python for Data Science

    o   Setting Up Your Environment: Jupyter Notebooks, Anaconda, and IDEs

    o   Python Basics: Variables, Data Types, and Functions

    o   Libraries You'll Need: NumPy, Pandas, Matplotlib, and Scikit-learn

3. **Understanding Data: Types, Sources, and Collection**

    o   Types of Data: Structured vs Unstructured

    o   Data Sources: Databases, APIs, Web Scraping, and Public Datasets

    o   Importing Data into Python: CSV, Excel, and SQL

4. **Data Cleaning and Preparation**

- The Importance of Clean Data: Common Data Problems
- Handling Missing Values
- Dealing with Outliers and Duplicates
- Normalization and Standardization
- Practical Example: Cleaning a Sales Dataset

5. **Exploratory Data Analysis (EDA)**
    - Understanding Your Data: Descriptive Statistics
    - Visualizing Data: Histograms, Bar Charts, and Scatter Plots
    - Data Distributions and Correlations
    - Practical Example: Exploring a Housing Price Dataset

6. **Introduction to Statistics for Data Science**
    - Basic Statistical Concepts: Mean, Median, Mode, Variance, and Standard Deviation
    - Probability: Key Concepts and Distributions
    - Hypothesis Testing: p-values, t-tests, and Chi-Square Tests
    - Practical Example: Applying Statistics to a Customer Data Analysis

7. **Data Visualization with Matplotlib and Seaborn**
    - Why Visualization Matters in Data Science
    - Introduction to Matplotlib: Plotting Basics
    - Enhancing Visuals with Seaborn: Heatmaps, Pair Plots, and Box Plots
    - Best Practices for Data Visualization

- Practical Example: Visualizing Trends in Sales Data

8. **Introduction to Machine Learning**
    - What is Machine Learning? Supervised vs Unsupervised Learning
    - Simple Machine Learning Models: Linear Regression, k-Nearest Neighbors
    - Training and Evaluating Models
    - Overfitting and Underfitting: Model Optimization Techniques
    - Practical Example: Building a Predictive Model for Housing Prices

9. **Project 1: Predicting Housing Prices**
    - Project Overview
    - Data Collection and Cleaning
    - Exploratory Data Analysis
    - Building and Evaluating a Machine Learning Model
    - Improving Model Accuracy

10. **Project 2: Customer Segmentation Using K-Means Clustering**
    - Project Overview
    - Understanding Customer Data
    - Applying K-Means Clustering
    - Interpreting Clusters and Insights for Business Strategy

11. **Introduction to Data Science with R (Optional)**
    - Why Learn R? A Brief Introduction

- Setting Up R and RStudio
- Basic R Syntax and Data Manipulation
- A Comparison: Python vs. R for Data Science

12. **Next Steps in Data Science**
    - Where to Go After This Book
    - Resources for Further Learning: Online Courses, Books, and Communities
    - Building a Portfolio: Showcasing Your Work
    - Networking in Data Science: Conferences, Meetups, and Social Media

13. **Appendices**
    - Glossary of Key Terms
    - Further Reading and Resources
    - Data Sources for Practice
    - Code Cheat Sheets (Python, Pandas, Matplotlib)

This structure will provide beginners with a clear and practical guide to data science, helping them progress from understanding the basics to applying their knowledge through projects.

Chapter 1: Introduction to Data Science

What is Data Science?

Data science is a multidisciplinary field that involves using scientific methods, algorithms, and systems to extract insights and knowledge from structured and unstructured data. At its core, data science combines elements of mathematics, statistics, computer science, and domain expertise to analyze and interpret complex datasets, enabling data-driven decisions.

In simple terms, data science helps us make sense of large amounts of data by identifying patterns, predicting future trends, and offering actionable insights. This field goes beyond mere data analysis; it focuses on finding meaningful relationships within the data, building predictive models, and creating visualizations that communicate findings effectively.

Data science is a broad discipline that includes:

- **Data analysis**: Making sense of data through statistical methods.
- **Machine learning**: Building models that can learn from and make predictions based on data.
- **Data engineering**: Managing and preparing data for analysis.
- **Visualization**: Creating visual representations of data to communicate insights.

From predicting customer behavior to optimizing business operations, data science has applications across industries like healthcare, finance, marketing, retail, and technology. Whether it's recommending a movie on Netflix, suggesting a product on Amazon, or forecasting demand in supply chains, data science is at the heart of these innovations.

Why Data Science Matters

In today's data-driven world, organizations are generating more data than ever before. From transaction records and customer interactions to social media activity and sensor data, every business is flooded with information. However, raw data by itself is of little value without the tools and techniques to analyze it and turn it into actionable insights. This is where data science plays a crucial role.

Key reasons why data science matters:

1. **Informed Decision-Making**: Data science helps organizations make smarter decisions based on insights drawn from data, rather than relying on intuition or guesswork. Businesses can use data science to identify trends, forecast outcomes, and assess the impact of strategies.

2. **Efficiency and Automation**: By using algorithms to automate processes, data science helps optimize workflows and reduce the need for manual intervention. This can lead to significant savings in time and resources.

3. **Personalization**: Companies like Netflix, Spotify, and Amazon use data science to personalize user experiences. Data-driven recommendations create a tailored experience for each user, increasing satisfaction and engagement.

4. **Competitive Advantage**: Organizations that leverage data science can outperform their competitors. By understanding customer preferences, market

trends, and operational inefficiencies, businesses can make informed decisions that give them an edge.

5. **Solving Complex Problems**: Whether it's predicting disease outbreaks, identifying financial fraud, or improving supply chains, data science provides powerful tools to tackle complex, real-world challenges.

In short, data science enables businesses and individuals to harness the power of data, turning raw information into insights that drive success.

The Data Science Workflow: From Data Collection to Insights

The data science process involves several key stages that transform raw data into actionable insights. Let's take a look at the typical workflow:

1. **Data Collection**: The first step in any data science project is gathering data. Data can come from a variety of sources such as databases, web APIs, sensors, or even social media. The goal is to acquire the relevant data needed to solve the problem at hand.

2. **Data Cleaning**: Real-world data is often messy, incomplete, or inconsistent. Before any analysis can begin, the data must be cleaned and pre-processed. This involves handling missing values, correcting errors, and ensuring that the data is in a suitable format for analysis.

3. **Exploratory Data Analysis (EDA)**: Once the data is cleaned, it's time to explore it. EDA involves using statistical methods and visualizations to better understand the patterns, relationships, and trends within the data. This step helps identify what questions to ask and informs the direction of further analysis.

4. **Feature Engineering**: In this step, the data scientist creates new features (variables) that may improve the predictive power of models. Feature

engineering involves selecting or transforming existing data to help algorithms better capture underlying patterns.

5. **Modeling**: Here, machine learning or statistical models are applied to the data. Depending on the problem, different algorithms may be used, such as linear regression, decision trees, or neural networks. The model learns from the data and makes predictions or classifications.

6. **Model Evaluation**: After building the model, it needs to be evaluated to see how well it performs. This involves comparing the model's predictions against actual outcomes using metrics like accuracy, precision, and recall.

7. **Deployment**: Once the model is tested and refined, it can be deployed in a real-world setting. This could involve integrating the model into a software system, an app, or a dashboard for continuous use.

8. **Monitoring and Maintenance**: After deployment, the model should be continuously monitored to ensure it remains accurate and effective. Over time, as new data becomes available, models may need to be retrained or adjusted.

This workflow is iterative, meaning data scientists often loop back to earlier stages as they refine their models and analysis. By following this structured approach, data scientists ensure that the insights generated are both reliable and actionable.

Key Roles in Data Science: Data Scientist, Analyst, Engineer, and More

Data science is a team effort, and there are several key roles that contribute to the process. Understanding these roles can help you decide where your strengths lie and what career path you might want to pursue.

1. **Data Scientist**:

- The data scientist is the "jack of all trades" in the data science process. They are responsible for everything from data cleaning and analysis to building machine learning models and interpreting results. Data scientists combine programming skills, statistical knowledge, and domain expertise to deliver actionable insights. They often work closely with stakeholders to define the problem and recommend data-driven solutions.

2. **Data Analyst**:
    - Data analysts focus on extracting, cleaning, and analyzing data to provide insights that support business decisions. While they may not build advanced machine learning models, they are skilled in using statistical methods and visualization tools to make sense of data. Analysts often work in business intelligence, helping organizations understand trends and patterns in their operations.

3. **Data Engineer**:
    - Data engineers are responsible for building and maintaining the infrastructure that supports data collection and analysis. They design pipelines for collecting, storing, and processing large volumes of data. Their work ensures that the data is available, accessible, and organized for analysis by data scientists and analysts. Data engineers often work with technologies like SQL, Hadoop, and Spark.

4. **Machine Learning Engineer**:
    - Machine learning engineers specialize in implementing and deploying machine learning models at scale. They work closely with data scientists to turn models into production-ready systems. Their role involves fine-

tuning models, optimizing algorithms, and ensuring that models can handle large datasets in real-world applications.

5. **Statistician**:
   - Statisticians focus on the mathematical side of data science. They use advanced statistical methods to analyze data, design experiments, and build models. While their role overlaps with data scientists, statisticians often work in research or academia, providing the theoretical foundation for data-driven approaches.

6. **Business Analyst**:
   - Business analysts bridge the gap between data and business strategy. They use data to answer specific business questions, helping organizations understand how data can drive profitability, efficiency, and customer satisfaction. Their focus is more on interpreting and presenting data in a way that non-technical stakeholders can understand and act upon.

Each of these roles contributes to the overall data science workflow, and often, teams consist of individuals from each of these areas, working together to leverage data effectively. As you begin your journey into data science, you may find yourself drawn to one or more of these roles, depending on your skills and interests.

This chapter provides a solid foundation on the basics of data science, the importance of data science in today's world, the typical workflow, and the different roles involved in the field. Next, we will dive into the technical side of data science by setting up Python and exploring its essential libraries. Ready to get started? Let's go!

Chapter 2: Getting Started with Python for Data Science

Why Python? The Power of Python for Data Science

Python has become one of the most popular programming languages for data science—and for good reason. Its simplicity, versatility, and strong community support make it the go-to language for both beginners and experienced professionals in the field. But why exactly is Python the best choice for data science?

1. **Ease of Learning**: Python's straightforward syntax makes it an excellent language for beginners. You can focus more on solving problems rather than getting bogged down by complex syntax. This makes Python an ideal choice for those new to programming and data science alike.

2. **Versatility**: Python is a general-purpose language, meaning it can be used for a wide variety of tasks, from web development to automation to machine learning. Its flexibility means you can handle everything from data collection to analysis, and even deployment—all within the same language.

3. **Rich Ecosystem**: Python has a massive ecosystem of libraries and frameworks specifically designed for data science. Whether you're doing basic statistics or advanced machine learning, there's a library for it. Popular libraries like NumPy, Pandas, Matplotlib, and Scikit-learn make it easy to work with data, create visualizations, and build predictive models.

4. **Integration with Other Tools**: Python integrates well with other data science tools and platforms. Whether you're working with big data frameworks like Hadoop and Spark or integrating with APIs, Python's flexibility allows you to connect your workflows with ease.

5. **Community Support**: Python's large and active community is another key advantage. The open-source nature of Python ensures that there are plenty of resources, tutorials, and forums to help you troubleshoot problems or learn new techniques. The community also constantly updates and enhances the available libraries, keeping Python at the cutting edge of data science.

Because of these factors, Python is widely used in industries ranging from finance to healthcare to technology, making it an essential tool for anyone looking to start a career in data science.

Setting Up Your Environment: Jupyter Notebooks, Anaconda, and IDEs

Before diving into coding, it's important to set up your Python environment. The right tools will make your data science journey much smoother. Here are some of the most commonly used tools for Python in data science:

1. **Jupyter Notebooks**:
    - Jupyter Notebooks are an interactive computing environment that allows you to write and execute code in blocks or "cells." This makes it easier to test and debug your code step by step. One of the key benefits of Jupyter Notebooks is that you can mix code with text, visualizations, and markdown. This is extremely useful for documenting your work, sharing it with others, or even creating reports.

- To install Jupyter, you'll need to install Python first (more on this in a moment) or use a package manager like Anaconda that comes with Jupyter pre-installed.

2. **Anaconda**:
   - Anaconda is a distribution of Python specifically designed for data science and machine learning. It comes pre-packaged with popular libraries like NumPy, Pandas, and Scikit-learn, as well as Jupyter Notebooks. This is ideal for beginners because it simplifies the installation process.
   - By using Anaconda, you won't need to install each library manually, and you can manage multiple environments easily. It also includes Conda, a powerful package and environment manager that helps keep dependencies organized.

3. **IDEs (Integrated Development Environments)**:
   - If you prefer writing Python code in a more traditional editor, there are many powerful Integrated Development Environments (IDEs) to choose from. Some popular options for data science include:
     - **PyCharm**: A full-featured Python IDE with code completion, debugging, and package management features.
     - **VS Code**: A lightweight editor that, when combined with Python extensions, provides a clean and powerful environment for coding in Python.
     - **Spyder**: An IDE designed specifically for data science, offering features like variable exploration, a console for interactive execution, and debugging tools.

While Jupyter is perfect for experimentation and data exploration, IDEs are often preferred for writing more complex or production-level code.

Python Basics: Variables, Data Types, and Functions

Before diving into data science libraries, it's essential to understand the core features of Python. These basics will serve as the foundation for all your data science projects. Let's explore a few of the most important concepts:

1. **Variables**:
    - In Python, variables are used to store data. You don't need to declare the type of a variable in Python, as it is dynamically typed. For example:

python

x = 5 # An integer

y = 3.14 # A float (decimal number)

name = "Data Science" # A string

2. **Data Types**:
    - Python supports several basic data types, which you'll use frequently in data science:
        - **Integers**: Whole numbers (e.g., 5, 100, -23)
        - **Floats**: Numbers with decimal points (e.g., 3.14, -0.01)
        - **Strings**: Text data (e.g., "Hello, world!")
        - **Booleans**: True or False values (True, False)

Python also includes more complex data types like lists, dictionaries, and tuples, which are especially useful for organizing data.

3. **Functions**:
    - Functions are reusable pieces of code that perform specific tasks. Python has many built-in functions, and you can also define your own using the def keyword:

python

def greet(name):

return f"Hello, {name}!"

print(greet("Alice")) # Output: Hello, Alice!

4. Functions will be essential when working with larger datasets or when you need to break your code into manageable pieces.

Libraries You'll Need: NumPy, Pandas, Matplotlib, and Scikit-learn

Now that you have a basic understanding of Python, let's explore some of the most important libraries for data science. These libraries provide powerful tools for working with data, from performing mathematical operations to building machine learning models.

1. **NumPy**:
    - NumPy is the foundational package for scientific computing in Python. It introduces the powerful ndarray object, which allows for efficient storage and manipulation of large numerical arrays. NumPy also provides a wide range of mathematical functions that operate on arrays.
    - A simple example of using NumPy to create an array:

python

```python
import numpy as np

arr = np.array([1, 2, 3, 4, 5])
print(arr)
```

- NumPy is especially useful for numerical computing and is a building block for many other libraries.

2. **Pandas**:

    - Pandas is the go-to library for data manipulation and analysis. It introduces two primary data structures: **Series** (1D arrays) and **DataFrames** (2D tables). Pandas makes it easy to clean, transform, and analyze datasets.
    - Here's an example of loading data with Pandas:

```python
import pandas as pd

df = pd.read_csv("data.csv")
print(df.head())
```

- With Pandas, you can perform operations like filtering, grouping, merging, and aggregating data with minimal effort.

3. **Matplotlib**:

- Matplotlib is a powerful visualization library. It allows you to create a wide variety of static, animated, and interactive visualizations. Whether you need simple line charts, bar charts, or more complex figures, Matplotlib can handle it.
- Example of creating a simple plot:

```python
import matplotlib.pyplot as plt

plt.plot([1, 2, 3, 4], [1, 4, 9, 16])
plt.xlabel("X-axis")
plt.ylabel("Y-axis")
plt.title("Sample Plot")
plt.show()
```

4. **Scikit-learn**:
    - Scikit-learn is the most popular machine learning library in Python. It provides simple and efficient tools for data mining and data analysis. With Scikit-learn, you can easily build machine learning models like regression, classification, and clustering models.
    - Example of a simple linear regression model using Scikit-learn:

```python
```

```
from sklearn.linear_model import LinearRegression

import numpy as np


X = np.array([[1], [2], [3], [4]])

y = np.array([2, 4, 6, 8])


model = LinearRegression()

model.fit(X, y)


print(model.predict([[5]]))  # Output: 10
```

Now that you're familiar with the tools and libraries needed to start your data science journey, we'll move on to the next chapter, where we'll dive deeper into data manipulation using **Pandas**. Let's begin transforming and analyzing real-world datasets!

Chapter 3: Understanding Data: Types, Sources, and Collection

Data is at the heart of data science. Understanding the different types of data, where to find it, and how to import it into your Python environment is crucial to any data science project. In this chapter, we'll explore the types of data you'll encounter, common sources of data, and how to bring data into Python for analysis.

Types of Data: Structured vs Unstructured

1. Structured Data

Structured data refers to data that is organized in a predefined format, typically in rows and columns. It can be easily stored in databases or spreadsheets and is usually numerical or categorical. Examples of structured data include:

- **Spreadsheets**: Excel files with rows and columns
- **Databases**: SQL databases that store records in tables
- **CSV Files**: Data stored in Comma-Separated Values format

Key Characteristics:

- Highly organized and easily searchable
- Predefined fields (e.g., columns in a table)
- Suitable for relational databases like SQL

2. Unstructured Data

Unstructured data doesn't follow a specific format or structure and is often harder to store and analyze. Examples include text, images, audio, and video data. Despite being more challenging to work with, unstructured data often contains valuable insights, especially in industries like social media, marketing, and natural language processing.

Examples of unstructured data include:

- **Text data**: Emails, social media posts, or web pages
- **Media**: Images, videos, and audio recordings
- **Logs**: Data from sensors or website traffic

Key Characteristics:

- No predefined structure or organization
- Can contain text, images, audio, and other multimedia
- Requires specialized tools (e.g., Natural Language Processing, image processing) to analyze

---

Data Sources: Databases, APIs, Web Scraping, and Public Datasets

Once you know the type of data you're working with, the next step is sourcing it. Data can come from a variety of places, including databases, APIs, web scraping, and publicly available datasets. Each source has its own unique characteristics and methods for data extraction.

1. Databases

Databases are one of the most common sources of structured data. Relational databases (like MySQL, PostgreSQL, and SQLite) store data in tables, making it easy to query and retrieve information using SQL. Non-relational (NoSQL) databases like MongoDB store unstructured data, often in JSON-like formats.

To extract data from databases, you typically write **SQL queries** to select, filter, and sort data. Python has libraries (like sqlite3, SQLAlchemy, and pymysql) that allow you to connect to databases and import data directly into your Python environment.

2. APIs (Application Programming Interfaces)

APIs allow applications to communicate with each other. Many platforms—such as Twitter, Google, and financial data providers—offer APIs to access their data. APIs usually return data in **JSON** or **XML** format, which is easy to parse and work with in Python.

To interact with APIs in Python, you can use the requests library:

python

import requests

response = requests.get("https://api.example.com/data")

data = response.json()

API documentation is crucial, as it will guide you through the types of data available and how to format your requests.

3. Web Scraping

Sometimes, data isn't readily available through APIs, but you can extract it directly from web pages using web scraping techniques. Web scraping involves downloading web content (usually HTML) and extracting the desired information using tools like **BeautifulSoup** and **Scrapy** in Python.

Example of web scraping with BeautifulSoup:

python

```
from bs4 import BeautifulSoup
import requests

url = "https://example.com"
response = requests.get(url)
soup = BeautifulSoup(response.text, 'html.parser')

# Extract specific data from the webpage
data = soup.find_all('p')  # Example: all paragraphs
```

Note: Always check the website's **robots.txt** file and terms of service to ensure that web scraping is allowed.

4. Public Datasets

Many organizations and platforms provide free, publicly available datasets that you can use for analysis and experimentation. These datasets often come in CSV, Excel, or JSON formats. Some popular sources of public datasets include:

- **Kaggle**: A platform with datasets across various domains like healthcare, finance, and marketing.

- **UCI Machine Learning Repository**: A collection of datasets for machine learning and statistical analysis.

- **Government Websites**: Many government agencies provide datasets for public use (e.g., data.gov).
- **Google Dataset Search**: A tool to search for publicly available datasets.

Public datasets are a great way to practice your skills and experiment with real-world data. In most cases, you can download the dataset and load it directly into Python.

Importing Data into Python: CSV, Excel, and SQL

Once you've sourced your data, the next step is importing it into your Python environment for analysis. Python's data science libraries, especially **Pandas**, make this process straightforward.

1. Importing CSV Files

CSV (Comma-Separated Values) is one of the most common formats for structured data. It's widely used because of its simplicity and ease of use. You can import CSV files into Python using the Pandas library:

python

import pandas as pd

Load a CSV file into a DataFrame

df = pd.read_csv("data.csv")

Display the first few rows of the dataset

print(df.head())

The read_csv() function automatically parses the data into a Pandas DataFrame, which is a tabular data structure perfect for analysis.

2. Importing Excel Files

Excel is another popular format for structured data. Pandas provides a function to read Excel files as well:

python

```
# Load an Excel file
df = pd.read_excel("data.xlsx")

# Display the first few rows of the dataset
print(df.head())
```

If your Excel file has multiple sheets, you can specify which sheet to load using the sheet_name parameter.

3. Importing Data from SQL Databases

To import data from SQL databases, you can use Pandas in conjunction with a database connection library like sqlite3 or SQLAlchemy:

python

```
import sqlite3
```

```python
# Connect to an SQLite database
conn = sqlite3.connect("database.db")

# Load data from a SQL query into a DataFrame
df = pd.read_sql_query("SELECT * FROM table_name", conn)

# Display the first few rows of the dataset
print(df.head())

# Close the connection
conn.close()
```

This process works similarly with other relational databases like MySQL, PostgreSQL, and SQL Server, using the appropriate Python connectors.

In the next chapter, we'll explore how to **clean and preprocess data**, which is a crucial step before any analysis or modeling. By now, you should have a solid understanding of the types of data, where to source it, and how to bring it into your Python environment for further analysis. Let's move on to the next stage of the data science workflow: getting your data ready for analysis.

Chapter 4: Data Cleaning and Preparation

Once you've collected your data, the next crucial step in the data science process is to clean and prepare it for analysis. In its raw form, data is often messy, incomplete, or inconsistent. Data cleaning ensures that the information you're working with is accurate and reliable, setting a solid foundation for your analysis or modeling. In this chapter, we'll explore the importance of clean data, common issues that arise, and practical techniques for cleaning and preparing your dataset.

The Importance of Clean Data: Common Data Problems

Why Clean Data Matters

Data cleaning is essential because the quality of your analysis or machine learning model is directly tied to the quality of the data. Dirty or poorly prepared data can lead to inaccurate insights, faulty predictions, and unreliable conclusions. In fact, it's estimated that data scientists spend 80% of their time cleaning data.

Common data problems include:

- **Missing values**: Cells or fields with no data

- **Outliers**: Data points that are drastically different from the majority

- **Duplicated data**: Multiple identical records that can skew results

- **Inconsistent data**: Variations in data formats, spelling errors, or mixed data types
- **Irrelevant data**: Fields that do not contribute to the analysis and add unnecessary noise

Addressing these problems ensures that your dataset is accurate, complete, and in a consistent format for analysis.

Handling Missing Values

Missing data is one of the most frequent issues in datasets. There are several ways to handle missing values depending on the context and the dataset size.

1. Removing Missing Values

If the number of missing values is small and their absence doesn't significantly affect the dataset, you can simply remove the rows or columns with missing data.

python

```python
# Drop rows with missing values
df_cleaned = df.dropna()

# Drop columns with missing values
df_cleaned = df.dropna(axis=1)
```

2. Imputation

In many cases, removing data isn't ideal, especially if a large portion of your dataset has missing values. Instead, you can fill in missing values using **imputation**, which involves replacing them with estimated values, such as:

- **Mean**: Replace missing values with the mean of the column.
- **Median**: Replace missing values with the median value, especially for skewed distributions.
- **Mode**: Replace categorical data with the most frequent value.

Example of imputing with the mean:

python

```
# Replace missing values with the mean of the column
df['column_name'].fillna(df['column_name'].mean(), inplace=True)
```

For categorical columns, you can fill missing values with the most frequent category:

python

```
# Replace missing categorical values with the mode
df['category_column'].fillna(df['category_column'].mode()[0], inplace=True)
```

Dealing with Outliers and Duplicates

1. Outliers

Outliers are data points that are significantly different from the rest of the data. While some outliers might be legitimate, others can be the result of errors or anomalies.

Outliers can heavily influence models, especially in regression analysis, and may need to be removed or treated.

To detect outliers, you can use techniques like:

- **Boxplots**: A visual representation that shows the distribution of data and highlights outliers.
- **Z-scores**: A statistical measure that indicates how many standard deviations a data point is from the mean.

python

```
# Detect outliers using the Z-score method
from scipy import stats
import numpy as np

z_scores = np.abs(stats.zscore(df['numeric_column']))
df_cleaned = df[z_scores < 3]  # Keep only data points within 3 standard deviations
```

2. Duplicates

Duplicate entries are common when data is collected from multiple sources or through automated processes. Duplicate rows can distort your analysis, especially in tasks like counting or aggregating data.

To identify and remove duplicates in Pandas:

python

Check for duplicate rows

df.duplicated()

Remove duplicate rows

df_cleaned = df.drop_duplicates()

Normalization and Standardization

Data often needs to be **scaled** so that all variables are on a similar range, especially when working with algorithms that rely on distance measures, such as K-Nearest Neighbors or clustering algorithms.

1. Normalization (Min-Max Scaling)

Normalization scales the data to a range between 0 and 1. This technique is especially useful when the values of different features have varying ranges.

python

from sklearn.preprocessing import MinMaxScaler

scaler = MinMaxScaler()

df_normalized = scaler.fit_transform(df[['numeric_column']])

2. Standardization (Z-score Scaling)

Standardization transforms the data such that it has a mean of 0 and a standard deviation of 1. This method is particularly useful for datasets that follow a normal distribution.

python

```python
from sklearn.preprocessing import StandardScaler

scaler = StandardScaler()
df_standardized = scaler.fit_transform(df[['numeric_column']])
```

Choosing between normalization and standardization depends on your specific dataset and the algorithms you'll be using.

Practical Example: Cleaning a Sales Dataset

Let's walk through a practical example of cleaning a **sales dataset** that includes product sales data with columns like Product_ID, Price, Quantity_Sold, and Date_Sold.

Step 1: Import the Dataset

python

```python
import pandas as pd

# Load the sales dataset
df = pd.read_csv("sales_data.csv")
```

```python
# Display the first few rows
print(df.head())
```

Step 2: Handling Missing Values Let's assume the Price column has some missing values. We'll replace them with the mean price.

python

```python
# Replace missing prices with the mean value
df['Price'].fillna(df['Price'].mean(), inplace=True)
```

Step 3: Removing Duplicates Check for and remove any duplicate rows in the dataset.

python

```python
# Drop duplicate rows
df = df.drop_duplicates()
```

Step 4: Dealing with Outliers We'll use a boxplot to detect outliers in the Quantity_Sold column and remove any values that fall outside of three standard deviations.

python

```python
import matplotlib.pyplot as plt
import seaborn as sns
```

```python
# Create a boxplot to visualize outliers
sns.boxplot(df['Quantity_Sold'])
plt.show()


# Remove outliers using Z-score
from scipy import stats
import numpy as np


z_scores = np.abs(stats.zscore(df['Quantity_Sold']))
df_cleaned = df[z_scores < 3]
```

Step 5: Normalization Finally, we'll normalize the Price and Quantity_Sold columns so that they are on a similar scale.

python

```python
from sklearn.preprocessing import MinMaxScaler


scaler = MinMaxScaler()
df[['Price', 'Quantity_Sold']] = scaler.fit_transform(df[['Price', 'Quantity_Sold']])
```

Step 6: Save the Cleaned Dataset

python

Save the cleaned dataset to a new CSV file

df_cleaned.to_csv("cleaned_sales_data.csv", index=False)

By the end of this chapter, you should now understand the importance of clean data and be equipped with the tools to handle common data issues, such as missing values, outliers, and duplicates. In the next chapter, we'll dive into **exploratory data analysis (EDA)**, where we'll begin to uncover insights and trends from the cleaned dataset using visualizations and descriptive statistics.

Chapter 5: Exploratory Data Analysis (EDA)

After cleaning and preparing your data, the next step in the data science process is **exploratory data analysis (EDA)**. EDA allows you to get a better understanding of your data by summarizing its main characteristics, often using statistical graphics and other data visualization techniques. This chapter will guide you through descriptive statistics, data visualization, and understanding data distributions and correlations.

Understanding Your Data: Descriptive Statistics

Before jumping into visualizations, it's essential to grasp the basic statistical properties of your data. Descriptive statistics provide simple summaries about the dataset, offering insights into the data's central tendency, variability, and distribution.

Key metrics to consider include:

- **Mean (Average)**: The sum of all values divided by the number of values.
- **Median**: The middle value when the data is ordered.
- **Mode**: The most frequent value in the dataset.
- **Standard Deviation**: Measures the amount of variation or dispersion in the data.
- **Min/Max**: The smallest and largest values in the dataset.

- **Percentiles**: Provide insight into the data distribution, showing where a certain percentage of values fall below.

In Python, you can easily compute these metrics using Pandas:

python

```
import pandas as pd

# Load the dataset
df = pd.read_csv("data.csv")

# Summary statistics
print(df.describe())
```

The describe() function provides a quick overview of key descriptive statistics for numerical columns in your dataset.

Visualizing Data: Histograms, Bar Charts, and Scatter Plots

Data visualization is a powerful tool for understanding the distribution of your data and identifying patterns, trends, or outliers. Some of the most common plots used in EDA include:

1. Histograms

Histograms are useful for visualizing the distribution of a single variable by dividing the data into bins and counting the number of observations that fall within each bin.

This is particularly helpful for spotting skewness, uniformity, or multimodality in the data.

```python
import matplotlib.pyplot as plt

# Plotting a histogram
df['column_name'].plot(kind='hist', bins=20)
plt.title('Histogram of Column Name')
plt.xlabel('Values')
plt.ylabel('Frequency')
plt.show()
```

2. Bar Charts

Bar charts are useful for comparing categorical data. For example, you might want to visualize the count of different categories within a dataset.

```python
# Bar chart for categorical data
df['category_column'].value_counts().plot(kind='bar')
plt.title('Bar Chart of Categories')
plt.xlabel('Category')
```

plt.ylabel('Count')

plt.show()

3. Scatter Plots

Scatter plots help in visualizing the relationship between two continuous variables. For instance, you might want to see how the price of a house correlates with its size.

python

```
# Scatter plot
df.plot(kind='scatter', x='Column_X', y='Column_Y')
plt.title('Scatter Plot of Column X vs Column Y')
plt.xlabel('Column X')
plt.ylabel('Column Y')
plt.show()
```

Data Distributions and Correlations

Understanding Data Distributions

When performing EDA, it's essential to understand the distribution of your data. The shape of the data distribution provides insights into its nature, such as whether it follows a normal distribution, is skewed, or has multiple peaks.

- **Normal Distribution**: Data is symmetrically distributed around the mean.
- **Right-Skewed**: A majority of the data is concentrated on the left with a tail extending to the right.

- **Left-Skewed**: A majority of the data is concentrated on the right with a tail extending to the left.

You can visualize distributions using histograms or density plots:

python

```
# Density plot to visualize distribution
df['column_name'].plot(kind='density')
plt.title('Density Plot of Column Name')
plt.xlabel('Values')
plt.show()
```

Correlations Between Variables

EDA also involves identifying relationships between variables. **Correlation** measures the strength of a linear relationship between two variables and ranges from -1 to +1:

- **+1**: Perfect positive correlation (as one variable increases, so does the other).
- **0**: No correlation.
- **-1**: Perfect negative correlation (as one variable increases, the other decreases).

In Python, you can compute the correlation matrix to visualize the relationships between multiple variables:

python

```
# Correlation matrix
corr_matrix = df.corr()
```

```python
# Heatmap of the correlation matrix
import seaborn as sns
sns.heatmap(corr_matrix, annot=True, cmap='coolwarm')
plt.title('Correlation Heatmap')
plt.show()
```

This heatmap helps you quickly identify which variables are strongly correlated and might be worth further exploration.

Practical Example: Exploring a Housing Price Dataset

To put the concepts of EDA into practice, let's explore a **housing price dataset** that includes features such as house size, number of bedrooms, location, and sale price. Our goal is to understand the relationships between the variables and gain insights into the factors affecting housing prices.

Step 1: Load the Dataset

python

```python
# Load housing price dataset
df = pd.read_csv("housing_prices.csv")
print(df.head())
```

Step 2: Descriptive Statistics Begin by calculating summary statistics to get an overview of the dataset.

python

Descriptive statistics

print(df.describe())

This will give you the mean, median, standard deviation, and percentiles for numerical variables such as Size and Price.

Step 3: Visualize the Data Let's use histograms to explore the distribution of Price and Size.

python

Histogram for House Prices

df['Price'].plot(kind='hist', bins=30)

plt.title('Distribution of House Prices')

plt.xlabel('Price')

plt.ylabel('Frequency')

plt.show()

Histogram for House Size

df['Size'].plot(kind='hist', bins=30)

plt.title('Distribution of House Size')

plt.xlabel('Size (sq ft)')

plt.ylabel('Frequency')

plt.show()

Step 4: Scatter Plot for Price vs. Size To explore the relationship between house size and price, a scatter plot is a good starting point.

python

```
# Scatter plot of Price vs. Size
df.plot(kind='scatter', x='Size', y='Price')
plt.title('House Size vs. Price')
plt.xlabel('Size (sq ft)')
plt.ylabel('Price')
plt.show()
```

Step 5: Correlation Matrix Finally, let's compute the correlation matrix to examine the relationships between all numerical variables.

python

```
# Correlation matrix
corr_matrix = df.corr()


# Display correlation heatmap
sns.heatmap(corr_matrix, annot=True, cmap='coolwarm')
```

plt.title('Correlation Matrix of Housing Prices Dataset')

plt.show()

From this heatmap, you might observe strong correlations between certain features, such as house size and price, while other features may have weak or no correlation.

Through this practical example, you've now learned how to perform EDA on a real dataset. You've covered descriptive statistics, visualized the data, examined distributions, and explored relationships between variables. In the next chapter, we'll dive deeper into **data visualization techniques**, using more advanced tools and methods to create compelling visual stories from data.

Chapter 6: Introduction to Statistics for Data Science

Statistics is the backbone of data science, providing the mathematical tools to analyze and interpret data. Understanding basic statistical concepts is essential for making informed decisions based on data. In this chapter, we'll cover foundational statistics, probability theory, hypothesis testing, and explore a practical example where these concepts are applied to customer data analysis.

Basic Statistical Concepts: Mean, Median, Mode, Variance, and Standard Deviation

Before diving into more complex statistical techniques, it's essential to understand some core concepts:

- **Mean (Average)**: The sum of all values divided by the number of values. It represents the central tendency of the data.

python

```
mean_value = df['column_name'].mean()
```

- **Median**: The middle value of a dataset when arranged in ascending order. Unlike the mean, the median is not affected by outliers.

python

median_value = df['column_name'].median()

- **Mode**: The most frequently occurring value in a dataset.

python

mode_value = df['column_name'].mode()

- **Variance**: A measure of how far each value in the dataset is from the mean. It quantifies the spread of data.

python

variance_value = df['column_name'].var()

- **Standard Deviation**: The square root of the variance, providing a measure of the spread of the data in the same units as the data itself. A small standard deviation means the data points are close to the mean, while a large standard deviation indicates a wide spread.

python

std_dev = df['column_name'].std()

These metrics help you understand the distribution of your data and provide a foundation for more advanced statistical analysis.

Probability: Key Concepts and Distributions

Probability is the measure of how likely an event is to occur. It's a critical component of data science, as many machine learning algorithms rely on probabilistic methods.

Key probability concepts include:

- **Random Variables**: Variables whose values are outcomes of random phenomena.
- **Probability Distribution**: A function that provides the probabilities of all possible values of a random variable.

Common probability distributions in data science:

- **Normal Distribution (Gaussian Distribution)**: Symmetrical and bell-shaped, where most values cluster around the mean. Many natural phenomena follow a normal distribution.

python

```python
import numpy as np
import matplotlib.pyplot as plt

# Generating normal distribution data
data = np.random.normal(0, 1, 1000)
plt.hist(data, bins=30)
plt.title('Normal Distribution')
plt.show()
```

- **Binomial Distribution**: Used when there are only two outcomes (success or failure) in a series of independent trials. Example: flipping a coin.
- **Poisson Distribution**: Used for counting the number of events that happen in a fixed interval of time or space.

Understanding probability distributions helps you model real-world phenomena and form the basis for statistical inference.

Hypothesis Testing: p-values, t-tests, and Chi-Square Tests

Hypothesis testing is a fundamental concept in statistics, used to determine whether the results of a data analysis are statistically significant.

Key elements of hypothesis testing:

- **Null Hypothesis (H_0)**: A statement that assumes no effect or no difference exists.
- **Alternative Hypothesis (H_1)**: A statement that suggests a significant effect or difference exists.
- **p-value**: The probability of obtaining a result equal to or more extreme than what was observed, assuming the null hypothesis is true. A low p-value (typically < 0.05) indicates that the null hypothesis can be rejected.

Common tests for hypothesis testing:

1. **t-test**: Used to compare the means of two groups. For example, comparing the average sales between two regions.

python

```python
from scipy import stats

# Performing t-test
t_stat, p_value = stats.ttest_ind(df['group1'], df['group2'])
print(f"t-statistic: {t_stat}, p-value: {p_value}")
```

2. **Chi-Square Test**: Used to determine if there is a significant association between categorical variables. For example, testing the relationship between customer age groups and product preferences.

python

```python
from scipy.stats import chi2_contingency

# Example contingency table for chi-square test
contingency_table = [[10, 20], [15, 25]]
chi2, p_value, dof, expected = chi2_contingency(contingency_table)
print(f"Chi2 statistic: {chi2}, p-value: {p_value}")
```

By performing hypothesis testing, you can determine if the results of your analysis are meaningful or if they occurred by chance.

Practical Example: Applying Statistics to a Customer Data Analysis

Let's apply the statistical concepts we've discussed to a practical example involving customer data. Suppose you work for an e-commerce company, and you're tasked with analyzing customer purchasing behavior.

Step 1: Load the Dataset We'll work with a customer dataset containing features like customer age, annual income, and spending score.

python

```
import pandas as pd
df = pd.read_csv("customer_data.csv")
```

Step 2: Calculate Basic Statistics Begin by calculating the mean, median, and standard deviation for customer age and spending score.

python

```
# Descriptive statistics
mean_age = df['Age'].mean()
median_income = df['Annual Income'].median()
std_spending = df['Spending Score'].std()
print(f"Mean Age: {mean_age}, Median Income: {median_income}, Std Spending Score: {std_spending}")
```

Step 3: Visualize the Distribution of Spending Score To better understand customer spending habits, visualize the distribution of the Spending Score using a histogram.

python

```
df['Spending Score'].plot(kind='hist', bins=20)
plt.title('Distribution of Spending Score')
plt.xlabel('Spending Score')
plt.ylabel('Frequency')
plt.show()
```

Step 4: Hypothesis Testing Suppose you want to test whether younger customers (under 30) have significantly different spending habits compared to older customers (over 30). You can use a **t-test** to compare the average spending score between the two groups.

python

```
# Divide the data into two groups
younger_customers = df[df['Age'] < 30]['Spending Score']
older_customers = df[df['Age'] >= 30]['Spending Score']

# Perform t-test
t_stat, p_value = stats.ttest_ind(younger_customers, older_customers)
print(f"t-statistic: {t_stat}, p-value: {p_value}")
```

If the p-value is below 0.05, you can conclude that the spending habits of younger and older customers are statistically different.

Step 5: Chi-Square Test for Categorical Variables You may also want to test if there's an association between customer gender and spending categories (high or low spenders). A **Chi-Square test** can help with this.

```python
# Create a contingency table
contingency_table = pd.crosstab(df['Gender'], df['Spending Category'])

# Perform Chi-Square test
chi2, p_value, dof, expected = chi2_contingency(contingency_table)
print(f"Chi2 statistic: {chi2}, p-value: {p_value}")
```

By applying these statistical tests, you can uncover insights about customer behavior and validate the findings using rigorous methods.

In this chapter, you've learned about essential statistical concepts such as mean, median, and standard deviation, as well as the basics of probability and hypothesis testing. You also applied these concepts to a practical example of customer data analysis. In the next chapter, we'll dive into **data visualization techniques**, helping you present your data in a clear and insightful way.

Chapter 7: Data Visualization with Matplotlib and Seaborn

In this chapter, we'll explore one of the most important skills for any data scientist: **data visualization**. Visualizing data helps communicate complex patterns and trends in a way that's easy to understand, enabling you to convey insights clearly and effectively. We'll introduce two powerful Python libraries—**Matplotlib** and **Seaborn**—to help you create compelling visualizations. By the end of the chapter, you'll be able to create a variety of plots and use visualization best practices in your data science projects.

Why Visualization Matters in Data Science

In the world of data science, **visualization** serves multiple purposes:

- **Exploratory Analysis**: Allows you to uncover patterns, trends, and relationships in your data.

- **Communication**: Simplifies complex data, making insights easier to share with stakeholders or colleagues.

- **Decision Making**: Helps identify key metrics and insights that guide business or research decisions.

Effective data visualization can make your analyses more compelling and actionable, helping people make informed decisions quickly.

Introduction to Matplotlib: Plotting Basics

Matplotlib is one of the most widely used libraries for creating static, animated, and interactive visualizations in Python. It provides extensive plotting capabilities, from simple line plots to more advanced visualizations.

Key Components of Matplotlib:

- **Figure**: The overall window or page on which the plot is drawn.
- **Axes**: The actual plot area where the data is visualized.
- **Plot**: The graphical representation of data (e.g., line plot, bar plot).

Let's start by creating some basic plots using Matplotlib.

1. **Line Plot**: This type of plot is useful for showing trends over time, such as tracking sales growth.

python

```
import matplotlib.pyplot as plt

# Example data
months = ['Jan', 'Feb', 'Mar', 'Apr', 'May']
sales = [200, 250, 300, 350, 400]

# Create a line plot
```

```python
plt.plot(months, sales, marker='o')
plt.title('Sales Over Time')
plt.xlabel('Months')
plt.ylabel('Sales')
plt.show()
```

2. **Bar Plot**: Great for comparing different categories, like product sales across various regions.

python

```python
regions = ['North', 'South', 'East', 'West']
sales = [150, 200, 180, 220]

# Create a bar plot
plt.bar(regions, sales)
plt.title('Sales by Region')
plt.xlabel('Region')
plt.ylabel('Sales')
plt.show()
```

3. **Scatter Plot**: Useful for visualizing the relationship between two continuous variables, like advertising spend and sales.

python

```
# Example data
ad_spend = [100, 150, 200, 250, 300]
sales = [200, 230, 280, 350, 400]

# Create a scatter plot
plt.scatter(ad_spend, sales)
plt.title('Sales vs Advertising Spend')
plt.xlabel('Advertising Spend')
plt.ylabel('Sales')
plt.show()
```

Enhancing Visuals with Seaborn: Heatmaps, Pair Plots, and Box Plots

Seaborn is a Python visualization library built on top of Matplotlib. It provides more advanced and aesthetically pleasing plots with less code, making it great for **exploratory data analysis**.

1. **Heatmaps**: Useful for visualizing correlations between multiple variables, such as a correlation matrix of numerical data.

python

```
import seaborn as sns
```

```python
import numpy as np

# Generate example data
data = np.random.rand(10, 10)

# Create a heatmap
sns.heatmap(data, annot=True, cmap='coolwarm')
plt.title('Correlation Heatmap')
plt.show()
```

2. **Pair Plots**: This plot shows pairwise relationships in a dataset, often used for understanding distributions and correlations.

python

```python
# Load an example dataset
df = sns.load_dataset('iris')

# Create a pair plot
sns.pairplot(df, hue='species')
plt.show()
```

3. **Box Plots**: Great for showing the distribution of a dataset and identifying outliers. For example, analyzing the distribution of sales figures.

```python
# Example data
sns.boxplot(x='Region', y='Sales', data=df)
plt.title('Sales Distribution by Region')
plt.show()
```

Best Practices for Data Visualization

Good visualizations not only convey information but also follow key design principles. Here are a few **best practices** to keep in mind when creating plots:

1. **Clarity Over Complexity**: Don't overwhelm your audience with too much information. Keep your visualizations simple and focused on key insights.

2. **Use Appropriate Charts**: Choose the right type of plot for your data. For example, use a bar chart for categorical data and a line chart for continuous data.

3. **Label Your Axes**: Always label your axes and provide a meaningful title. This helps users understand what they are looking at without confusion.

4. **Limit the Use of Colors**: Use color to highlight important information, but avoid using too many colors. Stick to a consistent color palette.

5. **Avoid Misleading Scales**: Ensure that the axes of your plots are scaled appropriately to avoid distorting the information.

Practical Example: Visualizing Trends in Sales Data

Let's bring everything together in a practical example, where we'll visualize trends in a fictional **sales dataset**. We'll use both Matplotlib and Seaborn to create a series of plots that help us understand key insights from the data.

1. **Load and Explore the Data**

python

```
import pandas as pd

# Load the dataset
df = pd.read_csv('sales_data.csv')

# Preview the dataset
df.head()
```

2. **Line Plot for Monthly Sales Trends**

python

```
# Aggregate sales data by month
monthly_sales = df.groupby('Month')['Sales'].sum()

# Plot the trend
```

```
plt.plot(monthly_sales.index, monthly_sales.values, marker='o')

plt.title('Monthly Sales Trends')

plt.xlabel('Month')

plt.ylabel('Total Sales')

plt.show()
```

3. **Bar Plot for Regional Sales Comparison**

python

```
# Aggregate sales by region

regional_sales = df.groupby('Region')['Sales'].sum()

# Create a bar plot

plt.bar(regional_sales.index, regional_sales.values)

plt.title('Sales by Region')

plt.xlabel('Region')

plt.ylabel('Total Sales')

plt.show()
```

4. **Heatmap for Correlations Between Variables**

python

```python
# Compute correlations
corr_matrix = df.corr()

# Plot a heatmap
sns.heatmap(corr_matrix, annot=True, cmap='coolwarm')
plt.title('Correlation Heatmap')
plt.show()
```

5. **Box Plot to Identify Outliers in Sales Data**

python

```python
# Box plot for sales
sns.boxplot(x='Region', y='Sales', data=df)
plt.title('Sales Distribution by Region')
plt.show()
```

By following these steps, you've created several meaningful visualizations that help uncover trends and relationships in sales data.

In this chapter, you learned how to visualize data using Matplotlib and Seaborn. We explored various plots, from line charts and bar plots to more advanced visualizations like heatmaps and pair plots. We also discussed best practices for creating effective visualizations. In the next chapter, we'll dive into **building simple machine learning**

models, where you'll apply everything you've learned so far to make predictions using real-world data.

Chapter 8: Introduction to Machine Learning

Machine learning is one of the most exciting and transformative areas of data science, enabling computers to make predictions, classify data, and even learn from patterns in data without being explicitly programmed. In this chapter, we'll introduce the basics of machine learning, explore key types of machine learning, and build simple models to see how these concepts work in practice.

What is Machine Learning?

Machine learning (ML) refers to the ability of computers to learn from data and make decisions or predictions based on that data. Instead of following hard-coded instructions, machine learning algorithms identify patterns in data and use these patterns to generate insights or predict future outcomes.

Key Characteristics of Machine Learning:

- **Learning from Data**: Machine learning models improve their performance based on the data they are trained on.

- **Generalization**: A good machine learning model should generalize well to new, unseen data, not just the data it was trained on.

Supervised vs Unsupervised Learning

There are two main types of machine learning: **supervised** and **unsupervised learning**.

1. **Supervised Learning**: In supervised learning, the model is trained on a labeled dataset, meaning that each data point is associated with the correct output (or label). The goal is to learn a mapping from inputs to outputs.
    - **Example**: Predicting house prices based on features like square footage, number of bedrooms, and location.
    - **Common Algorithms**: Linear Regression, k-Nearest Neighbors, Decision Trees.

2. **Unsupervised Learning**: In unsupervised learning, the data does not have labels, and the goal is to identify hidden patterns or structures within the data.
    - **Example**: Grouping customers into segments based on purchasing behavior.
    - **Common Algorithms**: K-means clustering, Hierarchical Clustering.

Simple Machine Learning Models: Linear Regression, k-Nearest Neighbors

We'll now look at two simple and widely used machine learning models: **Linear Regression** and **k-Nearest Neighbors (k-NN)**.

Linear Regression:

Linear Regression is a supervised learning algorithm used for predicting a continuous value. The model assumes a linear relationship between the input variables (features) and the target variable.

Example: Predicting housing prices based on features like size, number of rooms, and location.

The equation for a linear regression model is:

$$Y = \beta_0 + \beta_1 X_1 + \beta_2 X_2 + \dots + \beta_n X_n$$

Where:

- Y is the predicted value (e.g., house price),
- $X_1, X_2, \dots X_n$ are the features (e.g., size, number of rooms),
- β_0 is the intercept, and $\beta_1, \dots \beta_n$ are the coefficients for the respective features.

k-Nearest Neighbors (k-NN):

The k-Nearest Neighbors algorithm is a simple, non-parametric method used for both classification and regression. In **k-NN regression**, the predicted value is based on the average value of the k-nearest data points. In **k-NN classification**, the predicted label is based on the majority label of the k-nearest neighbors.

- **Example**: Predicting housing prices based on the prices of neighboring homes.
- **How It Works**: The algorithm identifies the k nearest neighbors in the dataset and uses their known values to predict the target value for a new data point.

Training and Evaluating Models

Training a machine learning model involves feeding it data and allowing it to learn the relationship between input features and the target variable. Once the model is trained, we need to evaluate its performance using a test dataset, which contains new, unseen data.

Steps in Model Training:

1. **Split the Data**: Divide the dataset into training and testing sets (commonly 80% training, 20% testing).

2. **Train the Model**: Fit the model to the training data.

3. **Evaluate the Model**: Use the test set to evaluate the model's performance on new data.

Common Evaluation Metrics:

- **Mean Squared Error (MSE)** for regression models: Measures how close the predictions are to the actual values.

- **Accuracy** for classification models: Measures the percentage of correct predictions.

Overfitting and Underfitting: Model Optimization Techniques

One of the key challenges in machine learning is ensuring that your model generalizes well to new data, rather than simply memorizing the training data. This leads us to two important concepts:

- **Overfitting**: Occurs when the model is too complex and captures noise in the data, leading to poor generalization to new data.

- **Underfitting**: Occurs when the model is too simple and fails to capture the underlying patterns in the data.

How to Address Overfitting and Underfitting:

- **Regularization**: Add penalties to the model to prevent overfitting. Common techniques include Lasso and Ridge regression.

- **Cross-Validation**: Use techniques like k-fold cross-validation to split the data multiple times and evaluate the model's performance across these splits.

- **Feature Selection**: Limit the number of features used in the model to avoid overfitting.

Practical Example: Building a Predictive Model for Housing Prices

Now that we've covered the basics of machine learning, let's apply what we've learned by building a **predictive model** to estimate housing prices based on various features like size, number of rooms, and location.

1. **Loading and Preparing the Data**

python

```python
import pandas as pd

# Load the housing dataset
df = pd.read_csv('housing_data.csv')

# Select relevant features and the target variable
X = df[['Size', 'Bedrooms', 'Location']]
y = df['Price']
```

2. **Splitting the Data**

python

```
from sklearn.model_selection import train_test_split

# Split the data into training and testing sets
X_train, X_test, y_train, y_test = train_test_split(X, y, test_size=0.2, random_state=42)
```

3. **Training a Linear Regression Model**

python

```
from sklearn.linear_model import LinearRegression

# Initialize the Linear Regression model
model = LinearRegression()

# Train the model on the training data
model.fit(X_train, y_train)
```

4. **Evaluating the Model**

python

```python
from sklearn.metrics import mean_squared_error

# Make predictions on the test set
y_pred = model.predict(X_test)

# Evaluate the model's performance
mse = mean_squared_error(y_test, y_pred)
print(f'Mean Squared Error: {mse}')
```

5. **Visualizing the Results**

python

```python
import matplotlib.pyplot as plt

# Plot the predicted vs actual housing prices
plt.scatter(y_test, y_pred)
plt.title('Actual vs Predicted Prices')
plt.xlabel('Actual Prices')
plt.ylabel('Predicted Prices')
plt.show()
```

Through this process, we've created a simple **Linear Regression model** that predicts housing prices based on the features of the home. We also evaluated the model's performance using **Mean Squared Error** and visualized the relationship between actual and predicted prices.

In this chapter, we introduced the fundamentals of machine learning, explored key concepts like supervised and unsupervised learning, and implemented simple machine learning models using **Linear Regression** and **k-Nearest Neighbors**. We also covered the importance of training and evaluating models and discussed common challenges like **overfitting** and **underfitting**. In the next chapter, we'll dive deeper into more advanced machine learning algorithms and explore techniques for improving model accuracy.

Chapter 9: Project 1 – Predicting Housing Prices

In this chapter, we'll apply the concepts covered so far by building a complete machine learning project from scratch. We'll predict housing prices based on various factors like size, number of rooms, and location. This hands-on project will guide you through the entire data science workflow, including data collection, cleaning, analysis, and model building.

Project Overview

In this project, you'll use real-world housing data to predict property prices. The goal is to create a **predictive model** that estimates house prices based on several features, such as square footage, the number of bedrooms, and the location of the property. Along the way, you'll perform **data cleaning**, **exploratory data analysis**, and build a machine learning model using **Linear Regression**.

Key Steps:

- **Step 1**: Collect and clean the data.
- **Step 2**: Explore and analyze the data.
- **Step 3**: Build a machine learning model.
- **Step 4**: Evaluate and optimize the model.

Data Collection and Cleaning

The first step in any data science project is collecting and preparing the data. For this project, we'll be using a publicly available **housing dataset**. You can either use a dataset from platforms like **Kaggle** or create a custom dataset using **web scraping** or **APIs**.

Importing and Cleaning the Data:

1. **Load the Dataset:**

python

```python
import pandas as pd

# Load the housing dataset
df = pd.read_csv('housing_data.csv')

# Display the first few rows
df.head()
```

2. **Check for Missing Values:**

python

```python
# Check for missing values
print(df.isnull().sum())
```

3. **Handle Missing Data**:

python

Drop rows with missing values (alternative: fill missing values with mean/median)

df.dropna(inplace=True)

4. **Convert Categorical Data** (e.g., converting location names to numeric values for the model):

python

df['Location'] = df['Location'].astype('category').cat.codes

At this point, we have a **clean dataset** ready for analysis. Next, we'll explore the data to gain insights and identify key patterns.

Exploratory Data Analysis (EDA)

EDA helps you understand the data, spot trends, and identify relationships between variables. In this step, we'll calculate some **descriptive statistics** and visualize the data using plots.

Step 1: Descriptive Statistics

python

Summary statistics for numerical columns

df.describe()

Step 2: Visualizing Data

1. **Histogram** to check the distribution of house prices:

```python
import matplotlib.pyplot as plt

plt.hist(df['Price'], bins=50)
plt.title('Distribution of House Prices')
plt.xlabel('Price')
plt.ylabel('Frequency')
plt.show()
```

2. **Scatter Plot** to see the relationship between house size and price:

```python
plt.scatter(df['Size'], df['Price'])
plt.title('House Size vs Price')
plt.xlabel('Size (sq ft)')
plt.ylabel('Price')
plt.show()
```

3. **Correlation Matrix** to understand relationships between features:

```python
import seaborn as sns

# Generate correlation matrix
correlation_matrix = df.corr()

# Plot heatmap
sns.heatmap(correlation_matrix, annot=True, cmap='coolwarm')
plt.title('Correlation Heatmap')
plt.show()
```

From the **correlation heatmap**, you can see which features (e.g., house size, number of bedrooms) have the strongest relationship with housing prices, which is valuable information for building the model.

Building and Evaluating a Machine Learning Model

Now that we've cleaned and explored the data, the next step is to build a machine learning model to predict housing prices. We'll start by using **Linear Regression**, a simple and effective model for this type of problem.

Step 1: Split the Data

We'll divide the data into a **training set** (to build the model) and a **testing set** (to evaluate its performance).

python

from sklearn.model_selection import train_test_split

Define the features (X) and target (y)

X = df[['Size', 'Bedrooms', 'Location']]

y = df['Price']

Split the data (80% train, 20% test)

X_train, X_test, y_train, y_test = train_test_split(X, y, test_size=0.2, random_state=42)

Step 2: Train the Model

Using **Linear Regression** to predict house prices.

python

from sklearn.linear_model import LinearRegression

Initialize the Linear Regression model

model = LinearRegression()

Train the model

model.fit(X_train, y_train)

Step 3: Evaluate the Model

We'll evaluate the model's performance using **Mean Squared Error (MSE)** and visualize the predicted vs actual prices.

python

```
from sklearn.metrics import mean_squared_error

# Make predictions on the test set
y_pred = model.predict(X_test)

# Calculate Mean Squared Error
mse = mean_squared_error(y_test, y_pred)
print(f'Mean Squared Error: {mse}')
```

Step 4: Visualize the Results

python

```
# Plot actual vs predicted prices
plt.scatter(y_test, y_pred)
plt.title('Actual vs Predicted Housing Prices')
plt.xlabel('Actual Prices')
```

plt.ylabel('Predicted Prices')

plt.show()

Improving Model Accuracy

After evaluating the initial model, we might find opportunities to improve its performance by **tuning hyperparameters**, adding more features, or using more advanced algorithms like **Random Forest** or **XGBoost**.

Techniques for Improving Accuracy:

1. **Feature Engineering**: Create new features from existing ones (e.g., price per square foot).

python

```python
df['Price_per_sqft'] = df['Price'] / df['Size']
```

2. **Regularization**: Use **Ridge Regression** or **Lasso Regression** to avoid overfitting.

python

```python
from sklearn.linear_model import Ridge

ridge_model = Ridge(alpha=1.0)
ridge_model.fit(X_train, y_train)
```

3. **Cross-Validation**: Use **cross-validation** to get a more robust estimate of the model's performance.

```python
from sklearn.model_selection import cross_val_score

scores = cross_val_score(model, X, y, cv=5)
print(f'Cross-validated scores: {scores}')
```

By experimenting with different techniques and models, you'll improve the accuracy of your housing price predictions and gain deeper insights into the data.

Conclusion

In this project, we walked through a complete **machine learning pipeline** for predicting housing prices. You've learned how to:

- Collect and clean data,
- Perform exploratory data analysis,
- Build and evaluate a machine learning model,
- And explore ways to optimize model performance.

This project equips you with foundational skills to tackle more complex data science challenges in the future. In the next chapter, we'll explore another hands-on project to deepen your understanding of machine learning and data science techniques.

Chapter 10: Project 2 – Customer Segmentation Using K-Means Clustering

In this chapter, we will explore an **unsupervised machine learning** technique called **K-Means Clustering**. The goal of this project is to segment customers into different groups based on their purchasing behavior. Customer segmentation is a powerful tool that businesses use to tailor their marketing strategies, personalize services, and improve customer retention. By the end of this project, you'll be able to identify distinct customer segments and extract valuable insights that can inform business decisions.

Project Overview

Customer segmentation is the process of dividing a company's customer base into groups of individuals who have similar characteristics or behaviors. This helps businesses understand their customer base better and design targeted marketing strategies. In this project, we'll use **K-Means Clustering** to segment customers based on features like **purchase frequency, total spending**, and **product categories**.

Key Steps:

- **Step 1**: Prepare and explore the customer dataset.
- **Step 2**: Apply the **K-Means** algorithm to cluster the data.
- **Step 3**: Evaluate and interpret the clusters.

- **Step 4**: Use the insights to suggest business strategies.

Understanding Customer Data

We will start by loading a **customer dataset** that contains relevant features for segmentation, such as **annual income, spending score, purchase history**, and **demographics**.

Step 1: Importing and Preparing the Data

python

```
import pandas as pd

# Load the customer dataset
df = pd.read_csv('customer_data.csv')

# Display the first few rows
df.head()
```

Step 2: Basic Data Exploration

Before applying the clustering algorithm, we'll perform some basic data exploration to understand the dataset.

python

```
# Check for missing values
print(df.isnull().sum())
```

```
# Summary statistics
df.describe()
```

Features for Segmentation

For this project, we'll focus on features that are important for customer segmentation:

- **Annual Income**: How much the customer earns annually.
- **Spending Score**: A score based on customer spending habits.
- **Age**: The customer's age, which can influence buying patterns.
- **Purchase History**: Number of purchases made by the customer.

Applying K-Means Clustering

K-Means is an algorithm that divides data into **K distinct clusters**. Each cluster represents a group of customers with similar attributes. We'll choose a value for K (the number of clusters) and assign each customer to a cluster based on their behavior.

Step 1: Data Preparation for Clustering

We'll scale the features so that all values are on a similar scale, which helps improve the performance of K-Means.

python

```python
from sklearn.preprocessing import StandardScaler

# Select relevant features for clustering
X = df[['Annual_Income', 'Spending_Score', 'Age']]

# Standardize the features
scaler = StandardScaler()
X_scaled = scaler.fit_transform(X)
```

Step 2: Choosing the Number of Clusters (K)

We can use the **Elbow Method** to find the optimal number of clusters by plotting the **Within-Cluster Sum of Squares (WCSS)** for different values of K.

python

```python
from sklearn.cluster import KMeans
import matplotlib.pyplot as plt

# List to store WCSS values for each K
wcss = []

# Test different numbers of clusters (K)
for k in range(1, 11):
```

```python
    kmeans = KMeans(n_clusters=k, random_state=42)

    kmeans.fit(X_scaled)

    wcss.append(kmeans.inertia_)


# Plot the WCSS values

plt.plot(range(1, 11), wcss)

plt.title('Elbow Method')

plt.xlabel('Number of Clusters (K)')

plt.ylabel('WCSS')

plt.show()
```

From the **Elbow Plot**, we choose the value of **K** where the WCSS begins to level off, indicating a good balance between the number of clusters and the quality of segmentation.

Step 3: Applying K-Means

Once we select the optimal K (e.g., K=3), we'll apply the K-Means algorithm to our data.

python

```python
# Apply K-Means with the selected number of clusters

kmeans = KMeans(n_clusters=3, random_state=42)

df['Cluster'] = kmeans.fit_predict(X_scaled)
```

```python
# Display the first few rows with cluster labels
df.head()
```

Each customer is now assigned to one of the three clusters.

Interpreting Clusters and Insights for Business Strategy

Once we've segmented the customers into clusters, the next step is to **analyze** each cluster to understand the characteristics of the customers in each group. This helps businesses tailor their marketing strategies and services to different customer segments.

Step 1: Visualizing the Clusters

We can use **scatter plots** to visualize how the clusters differ in terms of spending and income.

python

```python
import seaborn as sns

# Plot the clusters based on Annual Income and Spending Score
sns.scatterplot(x=df['Annual_Income'], y=df['Spending_Score'], hue=df['Cluster'], palette='Set1')
plt.title('Customer Segments Based on Income and Spending')
plt.xlabel('Annual Income')
```

plt.ylabel('Spending Score')

plt.show()

Step 2: Analyzing Each Cluster

We'll compute the **mean** of important features like **annual income** and **spending score** for each cluster to understand the profile of each segment.

python

```
# Calculate the mean for each cluster
cluster_means = df.groupby('Cluster').mean()
print(cluster_means)
```

Cluster Insights:

- **Cluster 1**: High-income, high-spending customers. These are premium customers that the business should target with exclusive offers and premium services.

- **Cluster 2**: Low-income, low-spending customers. These might be price-sensitive customers, and businesses can focus on discount strategies or budget-friendly products for them.

- **Cluster 3**: Middle-income customers with moderate spending habits. These customers might respond well to loyalty programs or targeted marketing campaigns.

Step 3: Tailoring Business Strategies

Based on the insights from the clusters, businesses can devise strategies to:

- **Target high-value customers** with personalized offers, premium services, and loyalty programs.

- **Engage price-sensitive customers** by offering discounts, promotions, or bundles.

- **Increase spending** for middle-tier customers by cross-selling or up-selling products that align with their needs.

Conclusion

In this project, you learned how to use **K-Means Clustering** for customer segmentation. You've segmented customers based on their income, spending habits, and other features, and used the insights to suggest business strategies that could help increase sales and customer engagement. Clustering is a powerful tool in data science that can be applied in various domains, from marketing to healthcare.

In the next chapter, we'll dive into more advanced machine learning algorithms and tackle more complex projects.

Chapter 11: Introduction to Data Science with R (Optional)

While Python is often the go-to language for data science, **R** has also cemented its place as a powerful tool for statistical analysis and data visualization. This chapter serves as an introduction to using R for data science and compares it to Python, helping you decide which language might be more suitable for your needs.

Why Learn R? A Brief Introduction

R was specifically developed for **statistical computing** and **data analysis**, making it a great choice for professionals working in fields like **biostatistics**, **econometrics**, and academia. R has a rich ecosystem of packages tailored for advanced data manipulation, modeling, and visualization.

Some key reasons to learn R for data science include:

- **Statistical Power**: R excels in statistical analysis and has numerous packages for specialized methods.

- **Data Visualization**: With libraries like **ggplot2**, R is renowned for producing high-quality, customizable visualizations.

- **Community and Support**: R has a large community of statisticians and data scientists who contribute to its vast ecosystem of packages.

Who Uses R?

- **Academics** and **researchers** in fields requiring complex statistical analysis.

- **Data scientists** in industries like healthcare, finance, and pharmaceuticals.

- **Businesses** looking to conduct detailed data analysis, such as market segmentation or customer behavior analysis.

Setting Up R and RStudio

To start working with R, you'll need to install two essential components: **R** itself, and **RStudio**, a popular integrated development environment (IDE) that makes coding in R easier and more intuitive.

Step 1: Installing R

Visit the **CRAN** website (https://cran.r-project.org) and download the latest version of R for your operating system (Windows, Mac, or Linux). Follow the installation instructions for your system.

Step 2: Installing RStudio

Once you have R installed, download and install **RStudio** from https://rstudio.com. RStudio provides a user-friendly interface with features like a console, script editor, and various tools for plotting and package management.

Step 3: Setting Up RStudio

After installing RStudio, open it, and you'll see the interface divided into several panes:

- **Script Editor**: For writing and editing code.

- **Console**: For running commands interactively.

- **Environment/History**: Shows the variables you've created and keeps track of your previous commands.
- **Plots/Packages/Help**: Displays visualizations, installed packages, and provides help documentation.

Basic R Syntax and Data Manipulation

Now that R and RStudio are set up, let's cover some **basic R syntax** to get you started with data manipulation.

Variables and Data Types

R supports several data types, including **vectors**, **matrices**, **data frames**, and **lists**.

```r
# Assigning variables
x <- 10
y <- "Data Science with R"
z <- c(1, 2, 3, 4, 5)  # A vector of numbers

# Checking variable types
class(x)  # Numeric
class(y)  # Character
class(z)  # Numeric vector
```

Data Frames

The **data frame** is the most common data structure used for datasets in R. You can create a data frame using the data.frame() function or import one from a file.

r

```
# Creating a simple data frame
data <- data.frame(
  Name = c("Alice", "Bob", "Charlie"),
  Age = c(25, 30, 35),
  Score = c(85, 90, 88)
)

# Viewing the data frame
print(data)

# Accessing columns
data$Name  # Access the "Name" column
```

Importing Data

You can easily import CSV or Excel files into R for analysis.

r

```r
# Importing a CSV file
data <- read.csv('data.csv')

# Viewing the first few rows
head(data)
```

Basic Data Manipulation

Common tasks like filtering, summarizing, and manipulating data can be done using **base R** or packages like **dplyr**.

```r
# Installing and loading dplyr
install.packages("dplyr")
library(dplyr)

# Filtering rows where age is greater than 25
filtered_data <- filter(data, Age > 25)

# Summarizing the data
summary(data)
```

A Comparison: Python vs. R for Data Science

Both Python and R are excellent choices for data science, but they have different strengths. Here's a comparison of the two languages:

Feature	Python	R
Ease of Learning	Beginner-friendly with clear, readable syntax.	Can have a steeper learning curve, especially for beginners.
Statistical Analysis	Good, but R is more specialized in statistics.	Best for complex statistical analysis and research.
Data Visualization	Libraries like Matplotlib and Seaborn are great.	ggplot2 and lattice offer advanced visualization capabilities.
Machine Learning	Excellent support through libraries like Scikit-learn and TensorFlow.	Some machine learning packages, but not as extensive as Python.
Community Support	Large, active community with extensive resources.	Strong community, especially for statistical applications.
Packages	Wide variety of packages for everything from ML to data manipulation.	Rich set of specialized packages for statistics and visualization.
Speed and Performance	Generally faster for large-scale data processing.	Can be slower for big data, but packages like data.table can help.

When to Use Python:

- You're working on projects involving **machine learning**, **AI**, or **deep learning**.

- You prefer a language that's more **general-purpose** and widely used in various domains.

- You're working in an environment that requires integration with web applications or large-scale systems.

When to Use R:

- You're focused on **statistical analysis**, research, or working in academia.

- You need advanced **data visualization** with customizable plots.

- You want to leverage the rich ecosystem of R packages tailored to specific types of analysis, especially in **biostatistics** or **economics**.

Conclusion

R is a powerful tool for data science, particularly in fields that require complex statistical analysis and visualization. While Python may be more versatile for general-purpose programming, R excels in areas like data exploration and statistical computing. By learning both languages, you can take advantage of their unique strengths and use them in tandem to tackle a wide variety of data science tasks.

In the next chapter, we'll explore advanced machine learning techniques, building on the foundational knowledge you've gained in this book.

Chapter 12: Where to Go After This Book

As you've now completed the foundational elements of data science, it's important to keep the momentum going. In this chapter, we'll discuss how to continue building your knowledge, create a portfolio to showcase your skills, and connect with the wider data science community. Data science is a fast-evolving field, and staying up to date is key to success.

Resources for Further Learning: Online Courses, Books, and Communities

Learning doesn't stop with this book. There are countless resources to help you dive deeper into specific topics or explore advanced areas like deep learning, big data, or specialized statistical methods. Here are some recommended avenues to further your learning:

Online Courses

- **Coursera** (Data Science Specializations from universities like Johns Hopkins and Stanford)

- **edX** (MIT, Harvard, and other prestigious schools offer courses on topics like machine learning and AI)

- **Udemy** (Courses for all skill levels, including Python, R, and machine learning)

- **Kaggle Learn** (Hands-on tutorials in data science and machine learning with real datasets)

Books

- *"Python for Data Analysis"* by Wes McKinney (A great resource for mastering data manipulation with Pandas)

- *"Data Science from Scratch"* by Joel Grus (Covers the basics of data science and Python programming)

- *"Hands-On Machine Learning with Scikit-Learn, Keras, and TensorFlow"* by Aurélien Géron (A practical guide to machine learning)

Online Communities

- **Kaggle**: A platform for competitions, datasets, and discussions about data science.

- **Stack Overflow**: A go-to forum for coding questions and troubleshooting.

- **Reddit**: Subreddits like r/datascience and r/machinelearning offer discussions, news, and learning resources.

- **Data Science Central**: A community hub for sharing insights, articles, and tutorials.

By engaging with these resources, you can continually enhance your skills and stay updated with the latest developments in the field.

Building a Portfolio: Showcasing Your Work

A well-structured portfolio is essential for anyone looking to break into data science. It demonstrates your abilities to potential employers and showcases the projects you've completed. Here's how to build a compelling portfolio:

What to Include in Your Portfolio:

- **Real-World Projects**: Include end-to-end projects that highlight your data collection, cleaning, analysis, and modeling skills. Projects like the housing price predictor and customer segmentation examples from this book would be great starting points.

- **Clear Documentation**: Ensure that each project is well-documented with a clear description of the problem, the approach you took, and the results you achieved.

- **Interactive Notebooks**: Share Jupyter or R Markdown notebooks with your code and visualizations, making it easy for others to follow your thought process.

- **GitHub Repository**: Host your code on GitHub to make it easily accessible. A clean and organized GitHub profile can impress employers and collaborators.

- **Blog Posts**: Writing about your projects or explaining data science concepts can demonstrate your ability to communicate technical topics effectively. Platforms like Medium or personal websites can host these articles.

Tools to Showcase Your Portfolio:

- **GitHub**: Perfect for sharing code and collaborating with others.
- **Kaggle**: You can upload your projects and share your notebooks with the Kaggle community.

- **Personal Website**: If you're comfortable, build a simple website using platforms like WordPress, Wix, or GitHub Pages to showcase your portfolio and projects in one place.

Networking in Data Science: Conferences, Meetups, and Social Media

Networking is a powerful tool for growing in your data science career. Connecting with other professionals can lead to new opportunities, mentorship, and collaborations.

Attending Conferences and Meetups

- **Data Science Conferences**: Events like Strata Data Conference, PyData, and AI & Big Data Expo are excellent opportunities to learn from experts, attend workshops, and meet fellow data scientists.

- **Local Meetups**: Sites like Meetup.com offer data science-focused events in most major cities. Participating in meetups allows you to connect with local professionals, share knowledge, and collaborate on projects.

Social Media for Data Scientists

- **LinkedIn**: Follow companies and thought leaders in data science, engage in discussions, and share your own projects to build your professional network.

- **Twitter**: Many data science experts share insights, tutorials, and the latest research on Twitter. Follow hashtags like #DataScience and #MachineLearning to stay updated.

- **Kaggle Discussions**: Participate in the Kaggle forums to engage with like-minded individuals and seek advice on solving data science challenges.

Mentorship and Collaboration

- **Find a Mentor**: Connecting with a mentor who's experienced in data science can provide you with guidance, help you troubleshoot complex problems, and offer career advice.

- **Collaborate on Projects**: Working on group projects or open-source contributions can expand your experience and improve your team collaboration skills.

Conclusion

Data science is a journey, and this book has given you a solid foundation to get started. Now, it's up to you to continue learning, practice with real-world projects, and network with others in the field. By constantly seeking new knowledge, showcasing your work, and engaging with the data science community, you'll be well on your way to becoming a skilled and confident data scientist.

With the skills and resources you've gained here, the possibilities are endless. From analyzing business data to solving complex problems with machine learning, you're now equipped to tackle a wide range of challenges in the exciting world of data science. Good luck on your journey!

Appendices

Glossary of Key Terms

This section will help you understand important terms and concepts in data science, many of which were introduced in this book. These definitions will be useful for quick reference as you work through your data science projects.

- **Algorithm**: A sequence of steps or rules used to solve a problem, particularly in data processing and machine learning.

- **Data Cleaning**: The process of correcting or removing incorrect, corrupt, or incomplete data from a dataset.

- **DataFrame**: A two-dimensional, table-like data structure in Pandas, similar to an Excel spreadsheet, used for data manipulation.

- **Feature**: An individual measurable property or characteristic used in data analysis or machine learning models.

- **Hypothesis Testing**: A statistical method that helps determine whether there is enough evidence in a dataset to support a certain hypothesis.

- **Machine Learning**: A subset of AI that allows computers to learn from and make decisions based on data.

- **Normalization**: Adjusting data to ensure it fits within a specific range or distribution, often used in preparing data for machine learning.

- **Outlier**: A data point significantly different from other observations in a dataset.

- **Overfitting**: A modeling error in machine learning where a model is too closely fitted to a specific set of data, leading to poor generalization on new data.

- **Standard Deviation**: A measure of the amount of variation or dispersion in a dataset.

Further Reading and Resources

To deepen your knowledge and explore specialized topics in data science, here are some recommended books, websites, and platforms.

Books

- **"Python for Data Analysis"** by Wes McKinney: A must-read for mastering Pandas and data manipulation in Python.

- **"Hands-On Machine Learning with Scikit-Learn, Keras, and TensorFlow"** by Aurélien Géron: Ideal for diving deeper into machine learning techniques.

- **"Data Science from Scratch"** by Joel Grus: A beginner-friendly introduction to data science using Python.

Websites and Platforms

- **Kaggle**: A platform with competitions, tutorials, and datasets for hands-on learning.

- **DataCamp**: Offers interactive courses on Python, R, and data science topics.

- **Coursera**: Online courses from top universities on data science, statistics, and machine learning.

- **Towards Data Science**: A Medium publication that shares articles on the latest trends, tutorials, and insights in data science.

Data Sources for Practice

Working with real-world data is crucial for learning data science. Below are some sources where you can find datasets for practice and projects.

- **Kaggle Datasets**: A wide variety of datasets for data science competitions and individual projects.

- **UCI Machine Learning Repository**: One of the oldest and most popular collections of datasets for machine learning.

- **Google Dataset Search**: A tool for finding datasets across various domains.

- **Government Open Data**: Many governments, such as the U.S. and U.K., provide public datasets for research and analysis.

Code Cheat Sheets

To help you quickly reference key Python libraries and functions, this section provides cheat sheets for Python, Pandas, and Matplotlib. These can be printed and kept as handy guides while coding.

Python Basics

- **Variables**: x = 5

- **Functions**: def my_function():
- **Loops**: for i in range(10):
- **Conditionals**: if x > 5:

Pandas Cheat Sheet

- **Read CSV**: pd.read_csv('file.csv')
- **Create DataFrame**: df = pd.DataFrame(data)
- **Filter Data**: df[df['column'] > value]
- **Group By**: df.groupby('column').mean()
- **Missing Data**: df.fillna(0)

Matplotlib Cheat Sheet

- **Line Plot**: plt.plot(x, y)
- **Bar Chart**: plt.bar(x, y)
- **Scatter Plot**: plt.scatter(x, y)
- **Histogram**: plt.hist(data, bins=20)
- **Customize Plot**: plt.title('Title'), plt.xlabel('X-axis'), plt.ylabel('Y-axis')

These appendices will serve as valuable tools as you continue your journey in data science, helping you reinforce concepts, find new resources, and efficiently reference code as needed.

References

Below is a list of key references used to guide the concepts and techniques covered in this book. These resources will provide further reading and a deeper understanding of data science topics.

Books & Articles:

1. **McKinney, Wes.** *Python for Data Analysis.* O'Reilly Media, 2017.
    - A comprehensive guide to using Python and Pandas for data manipulation and analysis.

2. **Géron, Aurélien.** *Hands-On Machine Learning with Scikit-Learn, Keras, and TensorFlow.* O'Reilly Media, 2019.
    - This book offers a hands-on approach to machine learning and deep learning techniques.

3. **Grus, Joel.** *Data Science from Scratch: First Principles with Python.* O'Reilly Media, 2019.
    - A beginner-friendly introduction to the core concepts of data science, using Python from the ground up.

4. **Raschka, Sebastian, and Vahid Mirjalili.** *Python Machine Learning.* Packt Publishing, 2019.

- Covers advanced machine learning algorithms and techniques with practical examples using Python.

5. **Hastie, Trevor, Robert Tibshirani, and Jerome Friedman.** *The Elements of Statistical Learning: Data Mining, Inference, and Prediction.* Springer, 2009.
    - A more advanced book focusing on statistical learning and machine learning algorithms.

6. **Chollet, François.** *Deep Learning with Python.* Manning Publications, 2017.
    - This book covers deep learning and how to use Python's Keras library for building neural networks.

Online Courses & Tutorials:

1. **Coursera – Machine Learning by Andrew Ng**
    - A popular online course that introduces machine learning algorithms and their real-world applications.
    URL: https://www.coursera.org/learn/machine-learning

2. **Kaggle Learn**
    - Kaggle's educational platform offers tutorials and mini-courses on data science and machine learning.
    URL: https://www.kaggle.com/learn

3. **DataCamp**
    - Interactive online courses that teach data science, machine learning, and coding in Python and R.
    URL: https://www.datacamp.com

4. **Towards Data Science – Medium**

    o A popular publication that offers insights and tutorials on data science, machine learning, and AI.
    URL: https://towardsdatascience.com

Datasets:

1. **Kaggle Datasets**

    o A vast repository of datasets available for free for data science projects.
    URL: https://www.kaggle.com/datasets

2. **UCI Machine Learning Repository**

    o A collection of datasets for machine learning research.
    URL: https://archive.ics.uci.edu/ml/index.php

3. **Google Dataset Search**

    o A search engine designed to help find datasets across various domains.
    URL: https://datasetsearch.research.google.com

4. **Open Government Data**

    o Many government portals (e.g., data.gov) offer public datasets on a wide range of topics, useful for data science projects.
    URL: https://www.data.gov

This list will support further learning and exploration, providing valuable context and foundational material for aspiring data scientists.

www.ingramcontent.com/pod-product-compliance
Lightning Source LLC
Chambersburg PA
CBHW082249220526
45469CB00009B/2938